THE IPA FOR LANGUAGE LEARNING

An introduction to the International Phonetic Alphabet

Joshua Rudder

First edition 2010.

www.nativlang.com

Feedback may be directed to publications@nativlang.com.

Contents

Introduction

One of the most trying and rewarding aspects of learning another language is the struggle to master pronunciation and, ultimately, acquire a native accent. To simplify the task, it makes sense to have access to a way of accurately representing human speech. Modern writing systems are of minimal assistance – spelling in languages like English, French, Arabic and even Spanish covers up as much as it reveals about pronunciation.

We need a system in which one (and only one) symbol represents one specific sound. In other words, we need an exact and consistent correspondence between symbols and sounds. That system is called the International Phonetic Alphabet, or IPA. In short, the IPA allows you to transcribe speech sounds in any language with a high degree of accuracy.

Over the course of this workbook, you will learn to use the IPA in clear steps. You will begin by working with the features of individual vowels and consonants. Then, you will tackle the concepts of the phoneme and the allophone, which will help you understand speech sounds in the context of natural languages. From there, you will learn the makeup of syllables and, finally, of longer streams of speech like words and phrases.

I keep my explanations short and provide clear examples from English and other languages. Whenever I use an example from another language, I explicitly name the language and give a translation. The organization and formatting clearly distinguish titles, explanations, examples and exercises. A blank lined space beneath many examples allows you to practice copying or modifying IPA transcriptions in some cases and transcribing from scratch in others. Exercises counterbalance many explanations and provide simple experience relevant to the topic covered.

The first appendix offers ruled space for you to practice writing potentially unfamiliar IPA symbols. The second reviews basic and common IPA symbols for transcribing English and provides examples that highlight the pronunciation of each symbol. The third illustrates the basic anatomy of speech production to help you visually associate terminology with physiology. The last contains answers to the exercises. You will also find a short index at the end of the book.

This workbook stands on its own as a self-contained series of lessons on the IPA. It may also supplement general introductions to phonetics, phonology or any course that deals with the practical aspects of language learning.

Vowels

This section introduces common vowel sounds and teaches you to write each sound in IPA. For each vowel, a primary example is given in English followed by a secondary example in another language. At this point, all consonants included in the transcriptions are basic and easy to read.

Pay very close attention to pronunciation instead of spelling as you transcribe each vowel.

"I" type vowels

Pronounce these examples aloud, then copy the IPA.

English	IPA transcription	Foreign language	IPA transcription
seem	sim __________	zien *"to see"* *(Dutch)*	zin __________
bid	bɪd __________	ik *"I"* *(Dutch)*	ɪk __________
soon* *(Scottish English)*	syn __________	tu* *"you"* *(French)*	ty __________

* The vowel **y** is pronounced like "ee" in "seem" but with rounded (or puckered) lips.

"E" type vowels

Pronounce the following examples, then copy the IPA.

say	se __________	e *"and"* *(Italian)*	e __________
led	lɛd __________	è *"it is"* *(Italian)*	ɛ __________

Word	IPA	Copy	Word	IPA	Copy
about	əbawt	______	finden *"to find"* *(German)*	fɪndən	______

"A" type vowels

Pronounce the following examples, then copy the IPA.

Word	IPA	Copy	Word	IPA	Copy
hand	hænd	______	كتاب kitab *"book"* *(Standard Arabic)*	kitæb	______
aisle	aɪl	______	desata *"unties"* *(Spanish)*	desata	______
fall *(American)*	fɑl	______	les Pays-Bas *"the Netherlands"* *(French)*	lɛ pei bɑ	______
prod *(British RP)*	prɒd	______	كتاب ketāb *"book"* *(Farsi)*	ketɒb	______

"O" type vowels

Pronounce the following examples out loud, then copy the IPA.

Word	IPA	Copy	Word	IPA	Copy
of	ʌv	______	go dona *"badly"* *(Ulster Irish)*	gə dʌnə	______
law *(British RP)*	lɔ	______	só *"only"* *(Portuguese)*	sɔ	______
so	so	______	o povo *"the people"* *(Portuguese)*	u povu	______

"U" type vowels

Pronounce the following examples, then copy the IPA.

book	bʊk __________	куда (kudá) *"to where?"* *(Russian)*	kʊda __________
moon	mun __________	fou *"crazy"* *(French)*	fu __________

Exercise 1

Answers to this and every exercise may be found in Appendix C at the end of this workbook.

Identify and circle the number of vowel sounds in each of the following English words. After that, pronounce and transcribe the vowels. If you speak a nonstandard dialect, attempt to stay as close to standard English as possible *or* represent your local speech as accurately as possible.

1.	ago	1	2	3	________________
2.	grabbing	1	2	3	________________
3.	stood	1	2	3	________________
4.	blunder	1	2	3	________________
5.	sword	1	2	3	________________
6.	composite	1	2	3	________________
7.	phonetic	1	2	3	________________
8.	taught	1	2	3	________________
9.	arrested	1	2	3	________________
10.	thickened	1	2	3	________________

You are now familiar with many of the symbols used to write vowels. However, your understanding of the makeup and organization of vowels remains crude and vague: "a-type vowels" versus "u-type vowels". Let's consider more reliable ways of distinguishing vowels. The IPA identifies vowels by the components that play a part in producing them. These components of a vowel are called its *features*.

Height

Height can be understood in a straightforward way: consider the position of your jaw when you make a vowel sound. The jaw extends, or opens wider, when you pronounce the "a" in "father". This produces an *open* or *high* vowel. On the other hand, your jaw closes when you pronounce the "ee" in "seem", which produces a *close* or *low* vowel.

Another way to approach height is to pay attention to the distance between your tongue and the roof of your mouth. The tongue pulls away from the palate when making the open vowel in "far" but closes the gap when making the close vowel in "sing".

The following list separates out the IPA vowels we learned above based on their height. Return to the previous section to review any unfamiliar symbols.

close vowels	sim	syn	bɪd	bʊk	mun	
	______	______	______	______	______	
mid vowels	se	lɛd	əbawt	ʌv	lɔ	so
	____	______	________	____	____	____
open vowels	hænd	aɪl	fɑl	prɒd		
	_______	_____	_____	________		

Backness

Backness can, as the name suggests, relate to how far forward or back you place your tongue when you produce a vowel sound. The tongue pushes forward towards the teeth when pronouncing the "ee" in "seem", which is a *front* vowel. The tongue retreats backward when pronouncing the "a" in "father", an example of a *back* vowel.

The list below sorts the same IPA vowels we learned based on their backness. Again, refer to the previous section to review any unfamiliar IPA symbols.

front vowels		**central vowels**	**back vowels**	
sim	syn		mun	
bɪd			bʊk	
se			so	
lɛd		əbawt	ʌv	lɔ
hænd		aɪl	fɑl	prɒd

Organizing vowels by height and backness

Combining the features of height and backness allows you to pinpoint a specific vowel based on its component features. For example, the "a" in "father" is an *open back vowel*. With this knowledge, it's possible to arrange IPA vowels in a chart based on these two features.

	front	**central**	**back**
close	i y ɪ		ʊ u
mid	e ɛ	ə	ʌ ɔ o
open	æ	a	ɑ ɒ

Exercise 2

Give both the backness and the height of the vowel in the following English words.

1. love __________ __________
2. did __________ __________
3. knead __________ __________
4. rune __________ __________
5. bad __________ __________
6. chef __________ __________

OTHER FEATURES

While height and backness play key roles in distinguishing vowels, other features add further detail to the makeup of vowels.

To make certain vowel sounds, such as the "oo" in "soon", you round your lips. Other sounds are unrounded, like the "ee" in "seem". This feature of vowels is called *roundedness*. Pronounce the vowels in the previous section, and you will find that close and mid back vowels are often rounded, while front and central vowels are generally unrounded.

Consider a practical example of roundedness. The vowel represented by French "u" or German "ü" and the vowel in English "sing" are both close front vowels. However, the first vowel is rounded, but the second is unrounded.

rounded vowel		**unrounded vowel**	
dess**us** *"above" (French)*	dəs**y** ___________	s**ee**m	s**i**m ________
über *"over" (German)*	**y**bər ___________	ils d**i**sent *"they say" (French)*	i d**i**z ___________

Another feature that may distinguish vowels involves the passage of air through the nose. When you pronounce a vowel sound but push the air through your nose, the result is a nasal vowel. This feature is known as *nasalization*. Nasalization often occurs before nasal consonants like "n" and "m". For instance, some English speakers nasalize the "a" in "hand" in rapid speech.

nasal vowel		**oral vowel**	
w**an**d *(American)*	w**ɑ̃**d ________	w**a**d *(American)*	w**ɑ**d ________
on dit *"we say" (French)*	**õ** di _________	de l'**eau** *"some water" (French)*	də l**o** _________

A final feature worth considering here is the *length* of the vowel, which describes how long you hold the vowel. For instance, most English speakers hold out the vowel in "raw" longer than the vowel in "rot". Indeed, for many American English speakers, length is the only feature that distinguishes the vowel in "raw" from the vowel in "rot".

short vowel		long vowel	
rot *(American)*	**rɑt**	**raw** *(American)*	**rɑː**
	________		________
tu *"you"* *(French)*	**ty**	**über** *"over"* *(German)*	**yːbər**
	________		________

You will notice that our transcriptions up to this point have excluded long vowels where English speakers pronounce them. British English speakers pronounce "law" as **lɔː** and not simply **lɔ**. Similarly, English speakers that "drop their r's" typically lengthen vowels: "hard" comes out as **hɑrd** in the US but **hɑːd** in Britain. From this point on, our IPA will indicate long vowels both to increase the accuracy of our transliterations and to accustom you to recognizing vowel length.

Exercise 3

Give the conventional spelling for the following English words written in IPA. Then list every one of the above features that applies to each vowel.

	ruːd	*rude*	*long close back rounded vowel*
1.	stʌd	________	________
2.	stʊd	________	________
3.	hæ̃d	________	________
4.	hiːd	________	________
5.	ɪz	________	________
6.	ɑf	________	________

7. diːl ______________ ______________________________

8. dɛlt ______________ ______________________________

9. spæːn ______________ ______________________________

10. siːn ______________ ______________________________

11. rũːm ______________ ______________________________

12. piːs ______________ ______________________________

13. ɔːt ______________ ______________________________

14. piːz ______________ ______________________________

15. kwɪk ______________ ______________________________

When two vowels occur side by side in the same syllable, they form a diphthong. Although we will examine syllables later, it's time to include diphthongs in our IPA, since they play such a crucial role in many languages.

You will not need to learn any new symbols to begin transcribing diphthongs. When you listen carefully to English diphthongs like the "ou" in "about", you hear a sequence of two familiar vowels: **aʊ**. Pay close attention to diphthongs as you read and transcribe the words below. Consider that most English speakers pronounce the so-called "long vowels" as diphthongs.

s**a**fe	s**eɪ**f	ac**ei**te *"oil" (Latin American Spanish)*	as**ei**te ______
______			
s**o** *(British RP)*	s**əʊ** ______	n**eu**tro *"neuter" (Spanish)*	n**eu**tro ______
s**o** *(American)*	s**oʊ** ______	um p**ou**co *"a little" (Portuguese)*	ũ p**ou**ku ______

Diphthongs typically involve a main vowel plus a close (i-type or u-type) vowel. When the main vowel comes first, the vowels form a *falling* diphthong. When the main vowel comes second, the diphthong is *rising*. From this point on, our IPA will indicate diphthongs both to increase the accuracy of our transliterations and to accustom you to recognizing diphthongs.

Exercise 4

Identify, pronounce and transcribe every diphthong in the following English words.

1. hound ______
2. nine ______
3. say ______
4. aisle ______
5. Rome ______
6. aim ______

Consonants

Consonants have a different set of features that distinguishes them. First, notice where in your mouth you produce each consonant sound. Air passes through both lips when you pronounce the "b" in "back" but through your tongue and gum ridge when you pronounce the "s" in "sack". This feature, which identifies where in the mouth the sound is made, is known as *place of articulation*.

As with vowels, we will begin studying consonants by learning to write essential consonant sounds in IPA. Consonants are grouped below by their place of articulation from front (the lips) to back (the throat). An English example demonstrates each consonant sound, and this is paired with a secondary example from another language. Return to the previous chapter to review any unfamiliar vowels and pay very close attention to the pronunciation rather than the spelling as you transcribe each consonant.

Bilabial

To pronounce some consonants, you tense both lips and push air through them. Such consonants are *bilabial* with respect to place of articulation.

wo**m**an wʊ**m**ən

____

pond **p**ɑnd

____

big **b**ɪg

____

má
"evil"
(Portuguese) **m**a

____

la **p**eau
"skin"
(French) la **p**o

____

voz
"voice"
(Spanish) **b**os

____

ファン
fan*
"fan"
(Japanese) **ɸ**an

____

la **v**oz*
"the voice"
(Spanish) la **β**os

____

* These sounds are absent from English. To pronounce ɸ, keep your lips together as if to make a "p" but pronounce an "f" sound instead. Doing the same but pronouncing a "v" sound results in the consonant β.

Labiodental

Other consonants are pronounced by placing your teeth against your lips. These consonants are *labiodental* with respect to their place of articulation.

after	æftər	une fois *"once"* *(French)*	yn fwa
	________		________
of	ʌv	Wagen *"car"* *(German)*	vɑːgən
	________		________

Dental

Dental consonants are made by pressing your tongue against your teeth.

		antes* *"before"* *(Spanish)*	an̪t̪es
			________
thimble *(Indian English)*	t̪ɪmbəl	tonto* *"foolish"* *(Spanish)*	t̪on̪t̪o
	________		________
this *(Indian English)*	d̪ɪs	dame* *"give me"* *(Spanish)*	d̪ame
	________		________
thimble	θɪmbəl	hazlo *"do it"* *(European Spanish)*	aθlo
	________		________
this	ðɪs	estado *"state"* *(Spanish)*	est̪aðo
	________		________

* The consonants **n̪ t̪ d̪** are pronounced like **n t d**, but with your tongue against your teeth rather than the gum ridge. For example, placing your tongue as if to pronounce "th" in "thing" but producing a "t" sound instead results in **t̪**.

Alveolar

Alveolar consonants are pronounced by pressing your tongue against the gum ridge above and behind your upper front teeth.

knee	**ni:** ______________
steam	sti:m ______________
deed	**di:d** ______________
ask	æsk ______________
as	æ:**z** ______________
trill* *(Scottish English)*	**tr**ɪl ______________
rid *(Standard English)*	ɹɪd ______________
utter *(American)*	ʌɾəɹ ______________

nehme**n** *"to take" (German)*	**n**e:mə**n** ______________
tout ça *"all that" (French)*	**t**u sa ______________
derb *"uncouth" (German)*	**d**ɛrp ______________
sain *"healthy" (French)*	**s**ɛ̃ ______________
la ca**s**a *"the house" (Italian)*	la ka**z**a ______________
ca**rr**o *"car" (Spanish)*	ka**r**o ______________
pe**r**na *"leg" (Caipira Portuguese)*	pɛ**ɹ**nə ______________
a**r**a**r** *"to plow" (Spanish)*	a**ɾ**a**ɾ** ______________

lead	li:d __________	lado *"side"* *(Portuguese)*	lad̪u __________
felt*	fɛɫt __________	alto *"tall"* *(Portuguese)*	aɫtu __________

* The trilled or rolled consonant **r** involves strong vibration of your tongue against the alveolar ridge. The "dark l" ɫ has a slight "w" sound and occurs in English whenever "l" precedes another consonant or a word break.

Postalveolar

When your tongue points a bit further back in your mouth, above and behind the gum ridge but still further forward than the roof of your mouth, you make a *postalveolar* consonant.

shelter	ʃɛɫtəɹ __________	quelque **ch**ose *"something"* *(French)*	kɛlk ʃoz __________
lei**s**ure *(British RP)*	lɛʒə __________	les **g**ens *"people"* *(French)*	lɛ ʒɑ̃ __________
i**tch**	ɪ**tʃ** __________	**c**'è *"there is"* *(Italian)*	**tʃ**ɛ __________
jest	**dʒ**ɛst __________	**g**ià *"already"* *(Italian)*	**dʒ**a __________

Palatal

Palatal consonants are made by pushing your tongue towards the hard palate on the roof of your mouth.

onion* *(rarely, in rapid speech)*	ʌɲən	____________
yes	jɛs	____________
dos años* *"two years" (Spanish)*	d̪os aɲos	____________
ya hay *"there already is" (Spanish)*	ja:j	____________
aglio* *"garlic" (Italian)*	aʎo	____________

* The consonants ɲ and ʎ are rarely heard in English. The sound of ɲ is not far from the "ny" in "canyon", while ʎ is like "lli" in "million". Both are pronounced quickly as one palatal sound.

Velar

When you press the body of your against the velum (soft palate) near the back of the roof of your mouth, you produce a *velar* consonant.

singing	siŋiŋ	____________
skim	skɪm	____________
good	gʊd	____________
loch* *(Scottish English)*	ɫɔx	____________
ngā whare *"the houses" (Māori)*	ŋa: faɾe	____________
caro *"expensive" (Spanish)*	kaɾo	____________
gagner *"to earn" (French)*	gaɲe	____________
خوب **khūb*** *"good" (Farsi)*	xu:b	____________

		qué hago* *"what do I do"* *(Spanish)*	ke a**ɣ**o ____________
west	**w**ɛst ____________	**oui** *"yes"* *(French)*	**wi** ____________

* The sounds **x** and **ɣ** pose a challenge for most English speakers. For **x**, hold your tongue firmly where you produce "c" in "caught" but pronounce the "h" in "home" instead. Do the same for **ɣ** but make sure the vocal chords in your throat vibrate, which produces a light gurgle.

Uvular

Uvular consonants are produced with the uvula dangling in the back of your throat.

		المنطقة al-manta**q**a* *"the region"* *(Arabic)*	al manta**q**a ____________
		قرمز **gh**ermez* *"red"* *(Farsi)*	**ɢ**eɾmez ____________
		raro* *"rare"* *(Brazilian Portuguese)*	**χ**aɾo ____________
		c'est **r**a**r**e* *"it's rare"* *(French)*	sɛ **ʁ**a**ʁ** ____________
		raro* *"rare"* *(European Portuguese)*	**ʀ**aɾo ____________

* Standard English does not contain uvular sounds. The consonants **q** and **ɢ** resemble **k** and **g** but are pronounced further back in the throat. The same applies to **χ** and **ʁ** which relate to **x** and

ɣ. The consonant ʀ resembles the alveolar trill (Spanish or Scottish trilled **r**) but is pronounced in the throat near the uvula rather than against the alveolar ridge.

Glottal

Glottal consonants are made at the base of your throat near the glottis (voice box).

uh-oh!*	ʔʌʔo: ____________	ʻohana* *"family"* *(Hawaiian)*	ʔohana ____________
hymn	**h**ɪm ____________	ro**j**o *"red"* *(Latin American Spanish)*	ro**h**o ____________
be**h**oove *(British RP)*	bɪɦu:v ____________	Pra**h**a *"Prague"* *(Czech)*	pra**ɦ**a ____________

* The glottal stop **ʔ**, sometimes described as a catch in the throat, is heard in English "uh-uh" (meaning "no!"). It's also articulated before initial vowels, as in "adding" **ʔæ:diŋ**. What's more, English speakers sometimes switch out **t** for a glottal stop, resulting in pronunciations like **hæʔ** for "hat" and, for some British speakers, **bɛʔə** for "better".

From this point on, our IPA will indicate glottal stops to increase the accuracy of our transliterations.

Exercise 5

Identify and transcribe every consonant in the following words. Then indicate the place of articulation of each consonant. Pay attention to pronunciation over spelling and refer to the examples above as needed.

1. act ___ ___ ___ ______________________________
2. ladder ___ ___ ___ ______________________________
3. wink ___ ___ ___ ______________________________

4. hauled ___ ___ ___ ______________________________

5. reason ___ ___ ___ ______________________________

6. every ___ ___ ___ ______________________________

7. ration ___ ___ ___ ______________________________

8. ridged ___ ___ ___ ______________________________

9. faced ___ ___ ___ ______________________________

10. using ___ ___ ___ ______________________________

11. houses ___ ___ ___ ______________________________

12. think ___ ___ ___ ______________________________

13. washed ___ ___ ___ ______________________________

14. bathes ___ ___ ___ ______________________________

15. aches ___ ___ ___ ______________________________

In the last section, I gave several notes with instructions to help you reproduce unfamiliar consonants in English. These notes asked you to position your tongue where you would pronounce one consonant but to pronounce another instead. This insinuates that consonants are not only made up of where you produce a sound, but also how you produce that sound. How you restrict airflow to produce a consonant is a feature known as *manner of articulation*.

Consider the same consonant sounds you just learned, this time grouped by manner of articulation and organized from most restricted to least restricted airflow. Return to the previous section to review any unfamiliar consonant symbols.

Nasal stop or nasal continuant

When you force air up through your nose to pronounce a consonant, the result is a *nasal*.

woman	wʊ**m**ən ________________
knee	**n**i: ________________
onion *(rarely, in rapid speech)*	ʔʌ**ɲ**ən ________________
singing	si**ŋ**i**ŋ** ________________

má *"evil"* *(Portuguese)*	**m**a ________________
a**n**tes *"before"* *(Spanish)*	a**n̪**t̪es ________________
neh**m**e**n** *"to take"* *(German)*	**n**e:mə**n** ________________
dos a**ñ**os *"two years"* *(Spanish)*	d̪os a**ɲ**os ________________
ngā whare *"the houses"* *(Māori)*	**ŋ**a: faɾe ________________

Oral stop or plosive

If you temporarily stop the airflow during a consonant sound, the resulting sound is a *plosive*.

pond	**p**ɑnd	______
big	**b**ɪg	______
thimble *(Indian English)*	**t̪**ɪmbəl	______
this *(Indian English)*	**d̪**ɪs	______
s**t**eam	s**t**iːm	______
dee**d**	**d**iː**d**	______
s**k**im	s**k**ɪm	______
good	**g**ʊd	______

la **p**eau *"skin"* *(French)*	la **p**o	______
voz *"voice"* *(Spanish)*	**b**os	______
ton**t**o *"foolish"* *(Spanish)*	**t̪**on**t̪**o	______
dame *"give me"* *(Spanish)*	**d̪**ame	______
tout ça *"all that"* *(French)*	**t**u sa	______
der**b** *"uncouth"* *(German)*	**d**ɛr**p**	______
caro *"expensive"* *(Spanish)*	**k**aɾo	______
gagner *"to earn"* *(French)*	**g**aɲe	______
المنطقة al-manta**q**a *"the region"* *(Arabic)*	al manta**q**a	______
قرمز **gh**ermez *"red"* *(Farsi)*	**ɢ**eɾmez	______

uh-oh!	ʔʌʔoː ____________	ʻohana *"family"* *(Hawaiian)*	ʔohana ____________

Fricative

If, instead, you severely restrict the airflow but do not stop it, you produce a *fricative*.

		ファン **f**an *"fan"* *(Japanese)*	**ɸ**an ____________
		la **v**oz *"the voice"* *(Spanish)*	la **β**os ____________
a**f**ter	ʔæ**f**tər ____________	une **f**ois *"once"* *(French)*	yn **f**wa ____________
o**f**	ʔʌ**v** ____________	**W**agen *"car"* *(German)*	**v**ɑːgən ____________
thimble	**θ**ɪmbəl ____________	ha**z**lo *"do it"* *(European Spanish)*	a**θ**lo ____________
this	**ð**ɪs ____________	esta**d**o *"state"* *(Spanish)*	est̪a**ð**o ____________
a**s**k	ʔæ**s**k ____________	**s**ain *"healthy"* *(French)*	**s**ɛ̃ ____________
a**s**	ʔæː**z** ____________	la ca**s**a *"the house"* *(Italian)*	la ka**z**a ____________

shelter	**ʃ**ɛɫtəɹ	________
lei**s**ure *(British RP)*	lɛ**ʒ**ə	________
lo**ch** *(Scottish English)*	ɫɔ**x**	________
hymn	**h**ɪm	________
be**h**oove *(British RP)*	bɪ**ɦ**u:v	________

quelque **ch**ose *"something"* *(French)*	kɛlk **ʃ**oz	________
les **g**ens *"people"* *(French)*	lɛ **ʒ**ɑ̃	________
خوب **kh**ūb *"good"* *(Farsi)*	**x**u:b	________
qué ha**g**o *"what do I do"* *(Spanish)*	ke a**ɣ**o	________
raro *"rare"* *(Brazilian Portuguese)*	**χ**aɾo	________
c'est ra**r**e *"it's rare"* *(French)*	sɛ ʁaʁ	________
ro**j**o *"red"* *(Latin American Spanish)*	ro**h**o	________
Pra**h**a *"Prague"* *(Czech)*	pra**ɦ**a	________

Affricate

An *affricate* is a sequence of sounds involving a plosive followed immediately by a fricative. Although written with multiple IPA symbols, it is treated as a single sound in a language. By consequence, what speakers of one language hear as an affricate, speakers of another language may hear as two distinct sounds.

itch **ʔɪtʃ**

____

jest **dʒ**ɛst

____

c'è
"there is"
(Italian)
tʃɛ

____

già
"already"
(Italian)
dʒa

____

grazia
"grace"
(Sardinian)
gɾa**ts**ja

____

zente
"people"
(Sardinian)
dzɛntɛ

____

Approximant

When you only lightly restrict airflow, the result is a more vowel-like sound called an *approximant*.

rid
(Standard English)
ɹɪd

____

yes **j**ɛs

____

west **w**ɛst

____

pe**r**na
"leg"
(Caipira Portuguese)
pɛ**ɹ**nə

____

ya ha**y**
"there already is"
(Spanish)
jaː**j**

____

oui
"yes"
(French)
wi

____

Trill

When the consonant sound involves a strong vibration, you produce a *trill*.

t**r**ill
(Scottish English)
t**r**ɪl

____

ca**rr**o
"car"
(Spanish)
ka**r**o

____

			raro *"rare"* *(European Portuguese)*	ʀaɾo __________

Flap or tap

When the consonant sound involves a single vibration, you produce a *flap*.

utter *(American)*	ʔʌɾəɹ __________	arar *"to plow"* *(Spanish)*	aɾaɾ __________

Lateral

If you force airflow around one or both sides of your tongue, the result is a *lateral* consonant.

lead	liːd __________	lado *"side"* *(Portuguese)*	lad̪u __________
felt	fɛɫt __________	alto *"tall"* *(Portuguese)*	aɫtu __________
		aglio *"garlic"* *(Italian)*	aʎo __________

Exercise 6

Return to the word list you analyzed in the previous exercise. This time, give the manner of articulation of each consonant.

1. act ___ ___ ___ ____________________
2. ladder ___ ___ ___ ____________________
3. wink ___ ___ ___ ____________________

4. hauled ___ ___ ___ ______________________

5. reason ___ ___ ___ ______________________

6. every ___ ___ ___ ______________________

7. ration ___ ___ ___ ______________________

8. ridged ___ ___ ___ ______________________

9. faced ___ ___ ___ ______________________

10. using ___ ___ ___ ______________________

11. houses ___ ___ ___ ______________________

12. think ___ ___ ___ ______________________

13. washed ___ ___ ___ ______________________

14. bathes ___ ___ ___ ______________________

15. aches ___ ___ ___ ______________________

The third and final essential feature of consonants is *voicing*, which determines whether or not the vocal chords vibrate when producing a sound. When the vocal folds in your glottis rapidly vibrate during a consonant, that consonant is *voiced*. When they do not vibrate, the resulting consonant is *voiceless*.

You can test whether or not a consonant is voiced by placing your fingers lightly against your throat while pronouncing that consonant. You will notice that your throat vibrates when you make a voiced consonant, but does not during a voiceless consonant.

Notice that some consonants have the same place of articulation and manner of articulation but differ in voicing. The consonant **z** in "zoom" and **s** in "sing" are both alveolar fricatives, but **z** is voiced and **s** is voiceless. In other words, **z** is the voiced counterpart of **s**, while **s** is the voiceless counterpart of **z**. They form a voiced/voiceless pair.

Consider a few more pairs of consonants that have the same place and manner of articulation but differ in voicing. Return to previous sections to review any unfamiliar IPA symbols.

voiceless consonant		voiced consonant	
sheep	**ʃ**i:p	plea**s**ure *(American)*	plɛ**ʒ**əɹ
	________		________
s**p**an	s**p**æ:n	**b**an	**b**æ:n
	________		________
s**t**ay	s**t**eɪ	**d**ine	**d**aɪn
	________		________

Exercise 7

Make a list of every IPA consonant symbol you have learned so far, separating them out into voiced/voiceless pairs. After that, match the words below so that each matched set contains at least one voiced/voiceless pair. Finally, identify the voiced/voiceless pair in each set of words.

1.	runs	crashed
2.	tints	of
3.	apple	grain
4.	ruined	rats
5.	the	adds
6.	lock	lab
7.	range	thing
8.	off	crutch
9.	shiny	nudging
10.	match	lesion

Although we have covered a wide range of consonant sounds, there are many subtle features of speech left unmentioned in the previous sections. In this section, we will consider four concepts that will help you increase the accuracy of your IPA consonant transcriptions.

First, notice that the initial **t** in words like "time" comes out with a puff of air, while the **t** in "s**t**op" does not. The inclusion of this subtle h-sound is known as *aspiration*. Aspiration is actually a type of *coarticulation*, since it involves the influence of one consonant sound on another. In IPA, we write coarticulated consonants in superscript next to the main consonant: **tʰ** in "time". From this point on, our IPA will indicate aspirated consonants.

aspirated consonant		unaspirated consonant	
po**p**	**pʰ**ɑ**pʰ**	s**p**y	s**p**aɪ
	________		________
ta**t**	**tʰ**æ**tʰ**	s**t**ay	s**t**eɪ
	________		________
kic**k**	**kʰ**ɪ**kʰ**	s**k**y	s**k**aɪ
	________		________

On a separate note, we have already considered the concept of vowel length, but haven't touched on the same phenomenon with consonants. Long consonants, also known as *geminate* consonants, are pronounced longer than their simple counterparts. We indicate gemination either with the long sign ː or by writing the consonant twice. Our IPA will indicate geminate consonants from now on.

single consonant		geminate consonant	
u**n**owned	ʔʌ**n**oʊnd	u**nkn**own	ʔʌ**n**ːoʊn
	________		________
un be**l** giorno *"a beautiful day"* *(Italian)*	um bε**l** dʒoɾno	be**ll**issima *"most beautiful"* *(Italian)*	be**ll**issima
	________		________

A further concept applies when we reconsider diphthongs, which you met earlier while studying vowels. Many of our transcriptions have included diphthongs, such as **ʌnoʊnd** and **ʌn:oʊn** above. However, in many languages and for many speakers, diphthongs can become more constricted, with the "i-type" sound pronounced as a consonant **j** and the "u-type" sound pronounced like **w**. For instance, some English speakers pronounce "though" **ðow** with a clear **w** sound instead of or alongside **ðoʊ** and **ðo**:.

diphthongs with vowels		**diphthongs with glides**	
unkn**ow**n	ʔʌn:**oʊ**n	unkn**ow**n	ʔʌn:**ow**n
	________		________________
s**ay**	s**eɪ**	s**ay**	s**ej**
	_________		_________

Finally, consider that there are times when less restricted consonants, particularly nasals, l-sounds and r-sounds, may play the part of a vowel in a syllable. Such sounds are called *syllabic consonants*. For instance, some American speakers pronounce "curve" without the vowel but with a strong "r" sound, like **k^hɹv**. This is indicated by writing a small line or understroke beneath the consonant: **k^hɹ̩v**.

Exercise 8

Write the following words in IPA, including at least one example of a diphthong with a glide in each transcription:

1. dime ________________ 2. steed ________________ 3. few ________________

Write the following words in IPA, including at least one example of a syllabic consonant in each transcription:

4. bird ________________ 5. little ________________ 6. person ____________________

Write the following words in IPA, including one example of aspiration in each transcription:

7. came ________________ 8. app ________________ 9. time _______________

Organizing Consonants by Their Features

Consonants are conventionally presented in a fairly straightforward chart. Such a chart allows you to identify individual consonants by place of articulation, manner of articulation and voicing. Left-to-right columns list places of articulation, from the front of the head to the back (lips to throat). Top-to-bottom rows list manners of articulation, from most to least restricted. Consonants are given in voiceless/voiced pairs at each intersection of place and manner.

	bilabial	**labiodental**	**dental**	**alveolar**	**postalveolar**	**palatal**	**velar**	**uvular**	**glottal**
nasal	m			n		ɲ	ŋ		
plos.	p b		t̪ d̪	t d			k g	q ɢ	ʔ
fric.	ɸ β	f v	θ ð	s z	ʃ ʒ		x ɣ	χ ʁ	h ɦ
approx.				ɹ		j	w		
trill				r				ʀ	
flap				ɾ					
lat.				l			ɫ		

Exercise 9

1. Identify the features that set the first consonant apart from the second in each pair below.

s / z ___*voicing (voiceless vs. voiced)*___

d / d̪ ____________________

ʔ / ɹ ____________________

t / θ ____________________

χ / ɢ ____________________

w / l ____________________

l / h ____________________

v / ɸ ______________________________

ŋ/w ______________________________

2. The consonant chart above has been somewhat simplified. For example, sounds can be made further down in the throat than **χ** or **ɢ**, but not as far down as the voice box. Where must we insert this information into the above chart?

3. The IPA uses the familiar symbols **t** and **d** to stand for alveolar plosives. Those symbols are modified to t̪ and d̪ to represent sounds with the same manner of articulation, but made against the teeth instead. Use the same logic, but start with **p** and **b**, to discover two symbols missing from the chart.

4. In Ancient Greek, θ spelled the sound /tʰ/ and ɸ spelled /pʰ/. Why might these aspirate stops make sense as a point of origin for the sounds θ and ɸ currently represent in IPA? Think carefully, and explain your analysis step by step.

Phonemes and Allophones

In the introduction I set a goal: to teach IPA as a way for language learners to represent speech sounds accurately, since existing writing systems fail to do so. Over the past two chapters, you've learned a series of symbols within what amounts to a more robust alphabet. In other words, our transcriptions still represent distinct sounds strung together, sound-by-sound, to form words. These distinct units of sound are known as *phonemes*.

house	haws	h - a - w - s	(four phonemes)
	____________		

Every symbol you have learned is up for grabs as a possible phoneme in a language. If we apply our understanding of phonemes to the everyday use of language, a further concept emerges. Consider the following examples.

conquest	kʰa**ŋ**kʰwɛstʰ	cone	kʰoʊ**n**
	____________________		____________
hotel	hoʊtʰɛ**ɫ**	love	**l**ʌv
	________________		____________

In the first pair of words, the **n** sound has two distinct outcomes. The phoneme **n** has two realizations here: **n** or **ŋ**, depending on context. English speakers do not hear these as two separate sounds but as two versions of the same sound **n**. We call **ŋ** and **n** *allophones* of the same single phoneme **n**. Likewise, the phoneme **l** has two allophones above: the allophone **ɫ** and the allophone **l**.

In examples like conquest/cone, we see that the distribution of **n**'s allophones depends on the context. The phoneme **n** has one allophone **ŋ** that shows up in some contexts (namely, before velar consonants) and another allophone **n** everywhere else. The two contexts are mutually exclusive: the first allophone will not appear where the second does, and the second allophone will not appear where the first one does. These allophones are said to be in *complementary distribution*.

potato	pʰətʰ**eɪ**tʰoʊ	potato	pʰətʰɑːtʰoʊ
	____________________		____________________

Something else happens in potato/potato. In this case, let's consider **eɪ** and **ɑ:** allophones of an underlying phoneme **a**. These two distinct allophones of **a** do not occur in different contexts. One can occur exactly where the other does. The two allophones are *free variants* in this context.

bad	**b**æ:d	**s**ad	**s**æ:d
	__________		__________

The **s** and **b** in the English words above are heard as two completely different sounds. In this case, **b** and **s** cannot be allophones of a single phoneme. Instead, they contrast one another. It follows that they are two different phonemes. We shall call these two sounds *contrastive*.

Exercise 10

Give English words containing sounds that illustrate the concepts you have just learned.

1. List two distinct phonemes in English and give an example of each phoneme.

2. List two allophones of one of the phonemes in your previous answer and give an example of each allophone.

3. Give three pairs of words in English following the rules below.

    i. In the first pair, include an example of two allophones in free variation. What is the underlying phoneme?

    ii. In the second pair, include an example of two allophones in complementary distribution. What is the underlying phoneme?

    iii. In the third pair, include an example of two contrastive phonemes.

Your transcriptions are becoming more detailed and complex. Ideally, you would have a way to indicate the beginning and end of your transcriptions. Moreover, you would be able to distinguish between a phonemic transcription versus an allophonic one. The IPA convention is to enclose phonemes in slashes /lajk ðɪs/ and allophones in brackets [laɪkʰ ðɪs].

transcriptions between slashes		**transcriptions between brackets**	
conquest	/kɑnkwest/	conquest	[kʰɑŋkʰwɛstʰ]
	________________		________________

As a rule of thumb, added details in allophonic transcriptions should not distinguish words, while the phonemes in phonemic transcriptions would if switched for other phonemes. For instance, [kʰɑŋkʰwɛstʰ] would not sound like a distinct word if pronounced [kɑŋkwɛst] without aspirated consonants. However, /kɑnkwest/ would be perceived as a different word (indeed, a nonsense word) if we switched the phoneme /k/ for /g/ to produce /gɑnkwest/.

Another way to understand the difference between the use of slashes and brackets is to consider the sounds between /slæʃəs/ as a *broad* transcription, and sounds between [bɹækɪts] as a *narrow*, more precise transcription. Notice that the more precise your transcriptions become, the less likely they are to match another transcription of the same word or phrase. Different transcriptions will represent different judgments about the speech of different speakers and even different dialects of a language.

From this point on, our IPA will include brackets or slashes as boundaries, which will increase the accuracy of our transcriptions and familiarize you with broad and narrow transcriptions.

Exercise 11

Return to your answers to the last exercise and enclose your transcriptions in slashes or brackets following the explanation you have just read.

Testing for Allophones and Phonemes

You have now learned the fundamentals of phonemes and allophones. You have even considered the kinds of contexts in which phonemes and allophones occur. At this time, you still need a way to determine—to test—whether or not two sounds count as two distinct phonemes or simply two allophones of the same phoneme in a language.

Phonemes and allophones initially seem like high-level concepts, but they only work when applied to sounds in a specific language. To find distinct phonemes in a language, we must identify pairs of distinct words that differ by one sound and one sound only.

night	/**n**ajt/	rite	/ɹajt/
	__________		__________
low	/**l**oʊ/	row	/ɹoʊ/
	__________		__________

The English word pair rite/night differs minimally, by one sound only. Such pairs of words that differ in one phoneme and one phoneme only are known as *minimal pairs*. Since English speakers hear /ɹaɪt/ and /naɪt/ as different words, it follows that they hear /ɹ/ and /n/ as two completely different sounds. Therefore, we conclude that /ɹ/ and /n/ are distinct phonemes in English.

Switching out [ɹ] for a trill sound [r] would result in a variant [raɪt]. In this case, [raɪt] and [ɹaɪt] are in free variation. Switching the allophone [n] in "night" for the alveolar allophone [ŋ] would produce the unacceptable pronunciation [ŋaɪt]. This second case exposes an example of complementary distribution, since English /n/ is pronounced [n] initially but [ŋ] before a velar plosive. In either case, English speakers hear these examples as allophones of /n/ and /ɹ/. It follows that allophones of a single phoneme are *non-contrastive*.

Crucially, minimal pairs allow us to determine the set of phonemes in one specific language. Another language could just as well conceive of [n] and [ɹ] as allophones of the same phoneme.

Exercise 12

1. First, list ten sounds you infer to be distinct phonemes in English.

2. Now list five minimal pairs in English that test if those ten sounds are different phonemes in English.

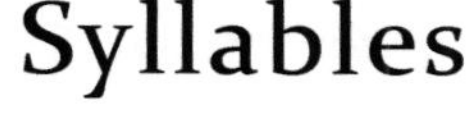

Syllables

You already have an understanding of phonemes, allophones, vowels and consonants. Assuming you thoroughly understood the previous chapters in this workbook, you already have the tools needed to build syllables out of sounds.

The core of a syllable is the vowel. This could be any vowel. Since vowels stand at the heart of a syllable, they are called the syllable *nucleus*.

hat [hæt^h] __________ ([æ] is the nucleus of the syllable)

damage [dæmɪdʒ] ______________ ([æ] is the nucleus of the first syllable and [ɪ] is the nucleus of the second)

Syllables are built by placing consonants around the vowel nucleus. The vowel includes long vowels and pure diphthongs (although diphthongs with glides like **j** and **w** may be treated as vowel + consonant or consonant + vowel sequences). Let us shorten "any vowel" to V. Similarly, let us shorten "any consonant" to C. Consonants may come before the nucleus, after the nucleus, or even both before and after the nucleus.

V	ah!	[ɑː]	______	([ʔɑː] = CV)
CV	do	[duː]	________	
VC	at	[æt^h]	__________	([ʔæt^h] = CVC)
CVC	had	[hæːd]	_____________	
(C)CCVCC(C)	splints	[splɪnts]	________________	

Exercise 13

Rewrite the following monosyllabic (single-syllable) words in English as strings of Cs (consonants) and Vs (vowels).

1. [stʌmp^h] _______________
2. [fjiw] _______________
3. [ʔown] _______________
4. [tʃuw] _______________
5. [speɪd] _______________
6. [daʊn] _______________

As mentioned, syllables are built around a nucleus. Consonants before the nucleus are part of the syllable *onset*. Consonants after the nucleus are part of the *coda* of a syllable. The nucleus and coda together form the *rhyme* of a syllable.

bad	b	-	æ:	-	d
ask	(0)	-	æ	-	sk
so	s	-	oʊ	-	(0)
	onset		**nucleus**		**coda**

Nucleus without a vowel

Earlier, you very briefly learned that some languages allow consonants to act like vowels in a syllable. In such cases, the consonant is the nucleus of the syllable and is written with a small understroke: "curve" (American English) **kʰɹ̩v**. Such consonants are known as *syllabic consonants*.

bird	[bɹ̩d]	_______________	(syllabic /ɹ/)
bottle	[bɑɾl̩]	_______________	(syllabic /l/)

Exercise 14

1. Return to the examples in the previous exercise. Circle the syllable onset and coda in each example.

2. Think of and write out three English words that may contain a syllabic consonant.

Two further observations are missing from our discussion of syllables. First, the makeup of syllables must be understood on a language-by-language basis, as a function of a specific language. Second, you do not yet have a way to represent syllables in your IPA transcriptions.

Restrictions on syllables

Languages have different constraints on the types of syllables they allow. As you saw in earlier examples, English permits a wide variety of syllables with a number of consonants both before and after the nucleus (consider the syllable [splɪnts]). Hawaiian, on the other hand, only allows syllables that end in a vowel.

ʻokina	*"glottal stop" (Hawaiian)*	/ʔo.ki.na/	________________
puke	*"book" (Hawaiian)*	/pu.ke/	________________

Transcribing syllables in IPA

IPA transcriptions may indicate syllables by inserting a visual break between symbols. The purpose of the IPA syllable symbol is to represent breaks between syllables. To accomplish this task, a low dot or period is placed between adjacent syllables.

wanting	[wʌn.tʰiŋ]	____________________
every	[ɛv.ɹij] or [ɛ.və. ɹij]	________________
representation	[ɹɛ.pɹij.zɛn.tʰeɪ.ʃən]	______________________________

Exercise 15

The standard spelling of Hawaiian vowels and consonants tends to match the IPA value (exception: ʻ = /ʔ/). A bar or "macron" above a vowel indicates that the vowel is long (ā = /aː/). Hawaiian syllables must end in a vowel but do not necessarily have an onset. Lastly, Hawaiian allows a wide variety of falling diphthongs ending in, for example, /e/ or /i/ or /u/.

Given that knowledge, write the following Hawaiian words in IPA. Include syllable breaks.

1. huna

____

2. ʻākeʻakeʻa

____

3. humuhumu-nukunuku-a-puaʻa

____

4. holoimua

____

5. walakīkē

____

6. Hawaiʻi

____

7. pāpā

____

8. kuaehu

____

9. Waikīkī

____

10. aloha

____

Words, Phrases, Utterances

You are familiar with phonemes, allophones and a range of consonants and vowels. You even have some understanding of units as large as a syllable. Now, how should you approach longer units of pronunciation like words, phrases and sentences?

Recordings of the human voice clearly demonstrate that people don't speak the way they write. We do not speak in words or sentences. Instead, we may pause between phrases or even in the middle of words. At the same time, our speech might flow straight over expected word and sentence breaks. This observation leads us to another new concept: a single continuous stream of speech known as an *utterance*.

This is an utterance. [ðɪs ɪz ən ʔʌɾəɹɪns]

Uh, so is, uhm, this… yeah. [ʔʌː soʊ ɪz ʔʌm ðɪs yæː]

Transcribing utterances

This concept of speech as streaming and continuous has ramifications for your IPA transcriptions. First, rapid speech does not distinguish word and sentence breaks. It follows that you do not use spelling conventions like spaces between words or punctuation in IPA without a good reason. You may use a period to separate syllables. You may decide to include spaces to help readers distinguish between words. Still, word spaces and syllable breaks are not essential to your transcription.

This transcription is legitimate. [ðɪs tʰɹæn.skʰɹɪp.ʃən ɪz lə.dʒɪ.tʰɪ.mətʰ]

And so is this one. [ʔæ̃nʔsoʊɪzðɪswən]

Assimilation

If speakers tend to produce speech as a stream of sound, it also follows that the barriers between sounds can easily blur. For this reason, sounds tend to become more like nearby sounds, a process known as *assimilation*. Consider an example introduced earlier.

conquest	kʰa**ŋ**kʰwɛstʰ	cone	kʰoʊ**n**
	____________________		____________

In the word pair conquest/cone, the phoneme /n/ has its expected outcome in [kʰoʊ**n**]. In the word [kʰa**ŋ**kʰwɛstʰ], /n/ takes on the place of articulation of the adjacent velar consonant /k/. Both [ŋ] and [kʰ] are velar consonants. In [kʰa**ŋkʰ**wɛstʰ], the phoneme /n/ *assimilates to* the following phoneme /k/.

With the concept of assimilation in hand, you can now begin to explain how phonemes could develop distinct allophones depending on context. Assimilation relies on the context surrounding a sound, more properly called its *environment*.

Exercise 16

1. Transcribe the five word pairs below as narrowly as you can in IPA.

   day / day**s** date / date**s** maid / maid**s** rake / rake**s** rag / rag**s**

   ____

   i. Identify the allophones of "plural –s" and the contexts in which they occur.

   ii. Identify the phoneme underlying "plural –s".

   iii. Make a rule that accurately predicts how to pronounce "plural –s" in any context.

2. Give the English spelling of the six words below, then answer the following questions.

[ʔɪmpʰʊtʰ] / [ʔɪntʰuː]   [hɛɫpt] / [hiːɫd]   [ʔiːziː] / [dʒʌst]

i. What is the underlying phoneme that varies in each pair?

ii. What are the allophones of each phoneme you found in (i.)?

iii. Which features differ among the allophones of each phoneme you found in (ii.)? In the first word in each pair, which nearby phoneme shares at least one of those features?

iv. What triggered assimilation in the first word in each pair? Describe the process step by step and include as much detail as possible.

Utterances show us that certain features apply at the level of words, phrases and sentences. These features take us beyond individual sounds and phonemes, so please review any and all unfamiliar symbols you have learned up to this point.

Accent

Many languages modify the pitch or volume of one or more syllables to distinguish them from surrounding syllables. This feature is known as *accent*.

Stress accent, often reduced to *stress*, involves one syllable (particularly the syllable nucleus) pronounced louder than surrounding syllables. Often, one syllable in a word is stressed, while others are unstressed, as in English "ho-**tel**" versus "**hos**-tel". This primary stress is transcribed in IPA with a straight apostrophe before the stressed syllable: [howˈ**tʰɛɫ**] vs. [ˈ**hɑs**təɫ]. Secondary stress is transcribed with a low apostrophe before the stressed syllable: [ˈtʰɛləˌ**fown**]. From this point on, our IPA transcriptions will indicate stress.

utterance [ˈʔʌ.ɾə.ɹɪns]

____

This is an utterance. [ˌðɪsɪzənˈʔʌɾəɹɪns] or [ˈðɪsˌʔɪzənˈʔʌɾəɹɪns]

____

Stress plays a crucial role in many languages. Consider a few examples from Spanish.

está	*"it is"(Spanish)*	[es.ˈt̪a]	_______________
ésta	*"this one"(Spanish)*	[ˈes.t̪a]	_______________
hablo	*"I speak"(Spanish)*	[ˈaβ.lo]	_______________
habló	*"(s)he spoke"(Spanish)*	[aβ.ˈlo]	_______________

Pitch accent, *intonation* or *pitch* involves one syllable (particularly the syllable nucleus) pronounced at a specific frequency. This could entail higher pitch, lower pitch or even complex pitch patterns. When transcribing pitch, you may use an acute accent for high or rising pitch (such as [á]) and a grave accent for low or falling pitch (like [à]).

端 (hashi) /ha.si/ *"border" (Japanese)* (even pitch)

箸 (hashi) /há.si/ *"chopsticks" (Japanese)* (high pitch on first syllable)

橋 (hashi) /ha.sí/ *"bridge" (Japanese)* (high pitch on last syllable)

Tonal languages

When pitch is used to contrast individual sounds, it is called *tone*. Languages that use pitch in this way are *tonal languages*. In tonal languages, tone applies at the level of individual sounds rather than longer units of speech like words or sentences. The most common examples of tone come from Chinese, including Mandarin and Cantonese. Notice that tones themselves contrast with one another in Chinese. When reading tones, try to imitate the sing-song quality of pitch.

割 (gē) *"divide" (Mandarin)* (high tone)

挌 (gé) *"fight" (Mandarin)* (rising tone)

舸 (gě) *" barge / boat" (Mandarin)* (falling-then-rising tone)

各 (gè) *"each / every" (Mandarin)* (falling tone)

Prosody

Prosody describes the application of features like accent to entire utterances and sentences. For instance, an English speaker may stress certain words or phrases in an utterance to emphasize them.

Are you ***finished***? ['ʔɑɾˌjuw'fɪ'nɪʃt] ____________________________

Are ***you*** finished? [ˌʔɑɾ'juwˌfɪnɪʃt] ____________________________

Well, ***are you***? [ˌwɛɫ'ʔɑɾ'juw] _________________________

Intonation may also apply at this level. For example, English speakers raise the pitch at the end of a question, but lower the pitch at the end of a declaration. Notice how these pitch changes are transcribed in IPA. Again, when reading pitch, try to imitate its sing-song quality.

Are you finished? [↗'ʔɑɾ↘ˌjuw↗'fɪnɪʃt] or [↘'ʔɑɾˌjuw↗'fɪnɪʃt]

____

You are finished. [↗'juw↘ˌʔɑɾ↗'fɪ↘nɪʃt]

____

Exercise 17

Read the following English utterances and transcribe them into IPA according to the instructions below.

"Uh-uh! That's not right!"

"Sorry, could you say that again?"

"The judge decided in favor of the plaintiff."

"I really miss her."

1. Transcribe the utterances as broadly as possible. Pay particular attention to phonemes.

____

____

____

____

2. Transcribe the utterances as narrowly as possible. Pay particular attention to allophones.

____

____

____

____

3. Add primary and secondary stress accents to your IPA. Think about the placement and weight of stress very carefully as you do this.

____

____

____

____

4. Add intonation arrows to your IPA. Think about the placement and level of pitch very carefully as you do this.

____

____

____

____

Exercise 18

Draw on everything you have learned to transcribe the following paragraph in IPA. Imitate American English pronunciation as much as possible.

"That wasn't a store robbery. That was an assassination. That wasn't a clerk. That was a wise guy. How do I know? I spent a little time with the FBI's organized crime unit. You could say that I'm intimately knowledgeable with the rancorous workings of the Mob in the Midwest section of this country… I'd look into it personally, but I got a date tonight."[1]

[1] *Career Opportunities*, dir. Bryan Gordon, Universal, 1991.

Exercise 19

Draw on everything you have learned to transcribe the following paragraph in IPA. Imitate British English pronunciation as much as is possible.

"But that he was not to be, without ignorance or prejudice, mistaken for a gentleman, my father most strongly asseverates; because it is a principle of his that no man who was not a true gentleman at heart, ever was, since the world began, a true gentleman in manner. He says, no varnish can hide the grain of the wood; and that the more varnish you put on, the more the grain will express itself."[2]

___

___

___

___

___

___

___

___

___

___

___

___

[2] Charles Dickens, *Great Expecations*, Planet PDF, http://www.planetpdf.com/planetpdf/pdfs/free_ebooks/Great_ Expectations_NT.pdf (accessed August 18, 2010), 319-320.

Extra

Take a trip to your local library or bookstore. While you're there, search for foreign language dictionaries (or other language reference books) that include IPA. Copy and pronounce the IPA transcriptions of at least thirty words from at least three separate languages (that is, ten words per language).

Appendix A: Copy Practice Worksheets

Writing practice for unfamiliar symbols

symbol

ε

name

epsilon / open e

type

Open-mid front unrounded vowel

ε

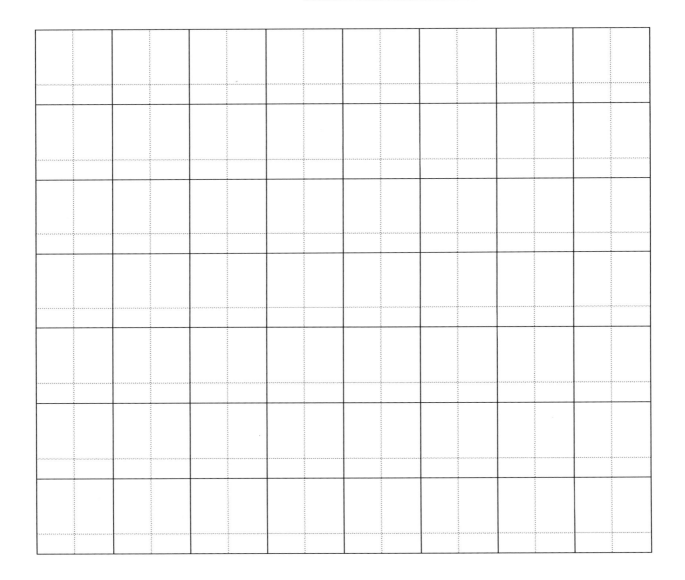

symbol

ə

name

s(c)hwa

type

Mid central vowel

ə

symbol

æ

name

ash

type

Near-open front unrounded vowel

symbol

ɑ

name

script a

type

Open back unrounded vowel

ɑ

symbol

ɒ

name

turned script a

type

Open back rounded vowel

symbol

ʌ

name

wedge / caret

type

Open-mid back unrounded vowel

ʌ

symbol

ɔ

name

open o

type

Open-mid back rounded vowel

ɔ

symbol

ʊ

name

upsilon / horseshoe

type

Near-close near-back rounded vowel

symbol

ɲ

name

left-tail n

type

Palatal nasal consonant

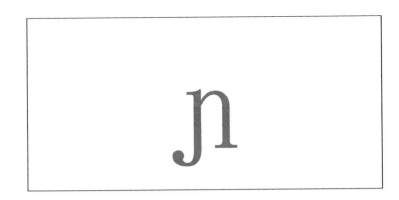

symbol

ŋ

name

eng(ma)

type

Velar nasal consonant

ŋ

symbol

ʔ

name

glottal stop

type

Voiceless glottal plosive consonant

symbol

ɸ

name

phi

type

Voiceless bilabial fricative consonant

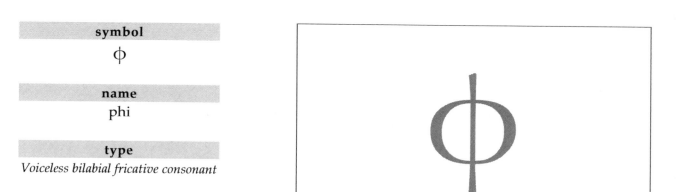

symbol

β

name

beta

type

Voiced bilabial fricative consonant

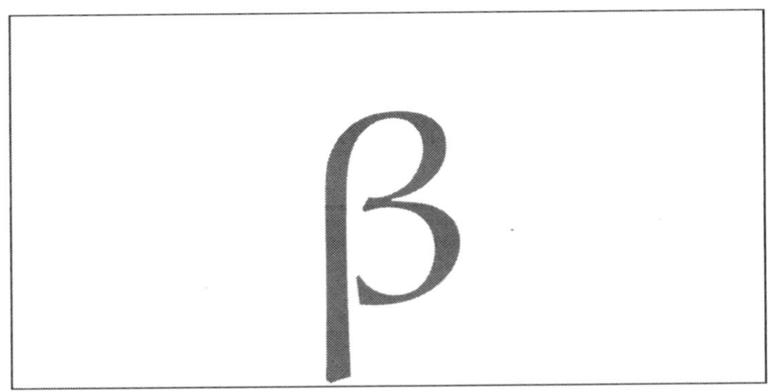

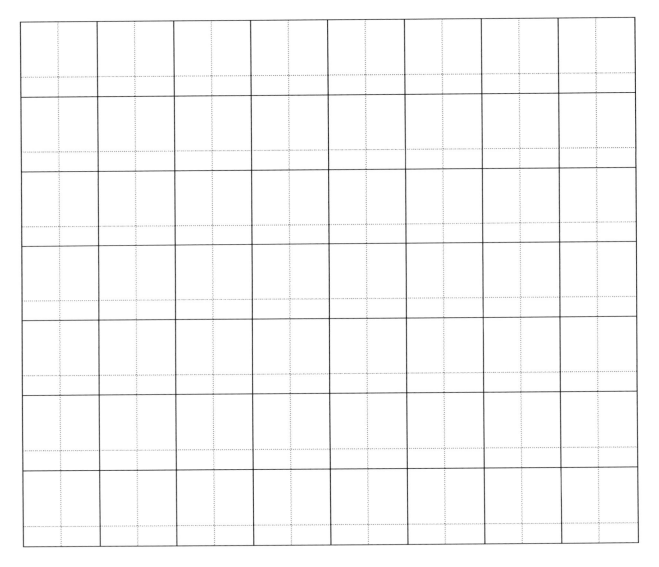

symbol

θ

name

theta

type

Voiceless dental fricative consonant

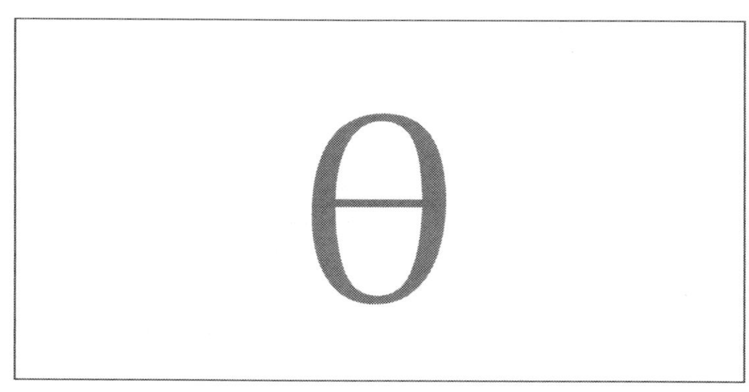

symbol

ð

name

eth / edh

type

Voiced dental fricative consonant

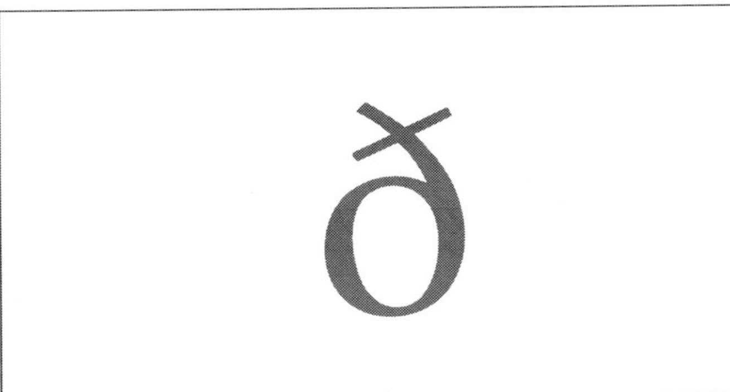

symbol

ʃ

name

esh

type

Voiceless palato-alveolar fricative consonant

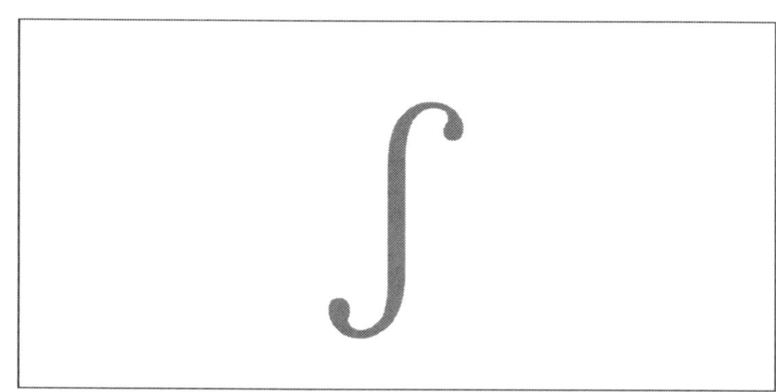

symbol

ʒ

name

ezh

type

Voiced palato-alveolar fricative consonant

ʒ

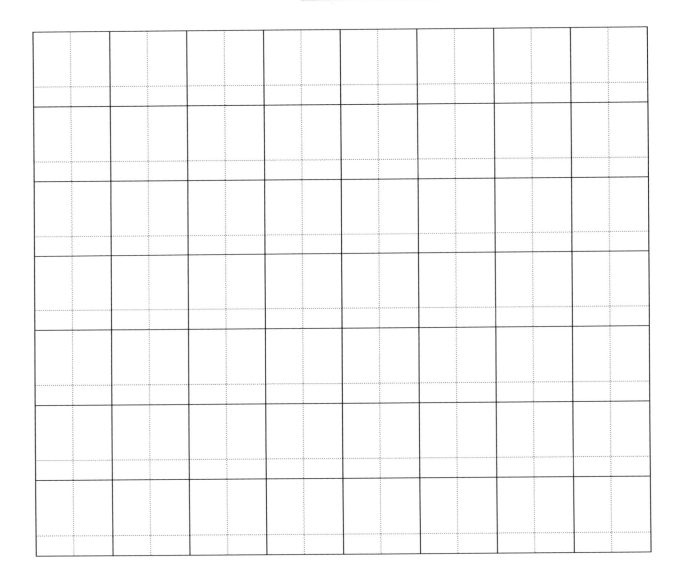

symbol

ɣ

name

gamma

type

Voiced velar fricative consonant

symbol

χ

name

chi

type

Voiceless uvular fricative consonant

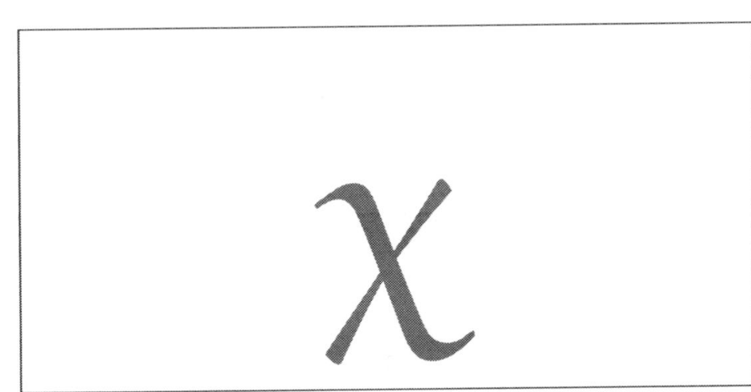

symbol

ʁ

name

inverted small capital r

type

Voiced uvular fricative consonant

ʁ

symbol

ɦ

name

hook-top h

type

Voiced glottal fricative consonant

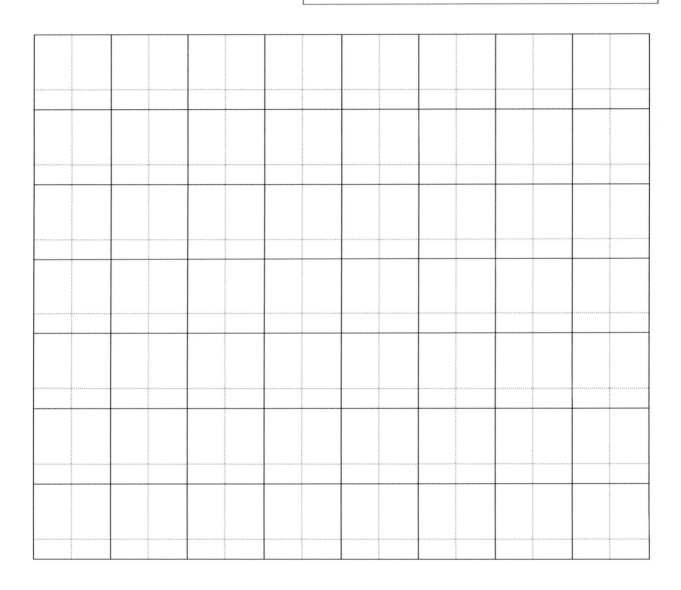

symbol

ɹ

name

turned r

type

Alveolar approximant consonant

ɹ

symbol

ɾ

name

fish-hook r

type

Alveolar tap consonant

ɾ

symbol
ʎ
name
turned y / palatal l
type
Palatal lateral consonant
ʎ

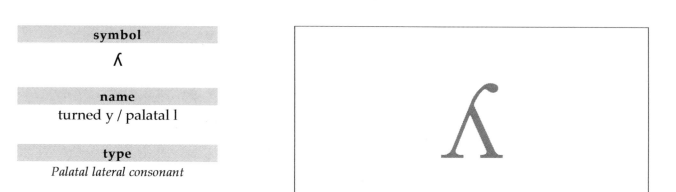

symbol

ɫ

name

dark l

type

Velarized alveolar lateral approximant consonant

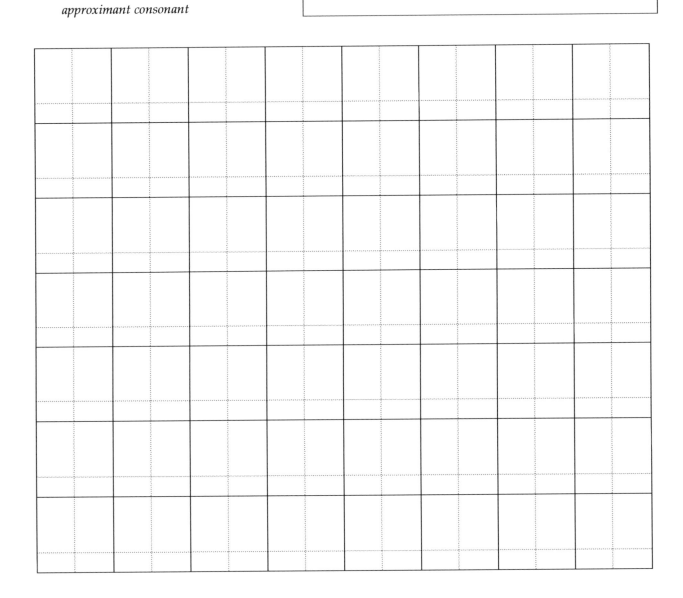

ɫ

Appendix B: Basic IPA for English

IPA symbols for transcribing English

Vowels

i — s**i**ng

ɪ — s**i**t

e — th**e**y

ɛ — l**e**t

ɜ — w**o**rd *(British)*

ə — **a**bout

æ — **a**sh

a — **a**isle

ɑ — f**a**ther

ɒ — n**o**t *(British)*

ʌ — c**u**p

ɔ — l**aw** *(British)*

o — t**o**w *(American)*

ʊ — b**oo**k

u — s**oo**n

Long vowels & nasal vowels

ː — after long vowel

- ɔː — l**aw** *(British)*

˜ — above nasal vowel

- ɑ̃ — fr**on**d *(through nose)*

Diphthongs

aɪ / aj — r**i**ght

eɪ / ej — s**ay**

ɔɪ / ɔj — t**oy** *(British)*

oɪ / oj — t**oy** *(American)*

aʊ / aw — **ou**t

əʊ / əw — s**o** *(British)*

oʊ / ow — s**o** *(American)*

Consonants

m — see**m**

n — sa**n**e

ŋ — si**ng**

p — s**p**ace

b — **b**ody

t — s**t**ay

d — **d**ash

k — s**c**ale

g — **g**ain

ʔ — uh**-**oh

f — **f**in

v — **v**enue

θ — **th**eme

ð thus

ʃ shoe

ʒ pleasure

tʃ chirp

dʒ judge

h home

ɹ raid

j yes

w woe

ɾ batter *(American)*

l loom

ɫ bulk

Aspirated consonants & geminates

ʰ after aspirated consonant

[tʰeɪkʰ] take

ː after geminate consonant

nː can nudge

Syllables

. between syllables

/i.vən/ **even**

ˈ before primary stressed syllable

[kəmˈ**baɪn**] com**bine**

ˌ before secondary stressed syllable

[ˌθɛɹəˈpʰjuːtʰɪkʰ] **the**rapeutic

↗ before syllable with rising pitch

[ɑɹ ↗juː] Are ***you?***

↘ before syllable with falling pitch

[juː ↘ɑɹ] You **are.**

IPA Vowel Chart (simplified)

	front	central	back
close	i y ɪ		ʊ u
mid	e ɛ	ə	ʌ ɔ o
open	æ	a	ɑ ɒ

IPA Consonant Chart (simplified)

	bilabial	labiodental	dental	alveolar	postalveolar	palatal	velar	uvular	glottal
nasal	m			n		ɲ	ŋ		
plos.	p b		t̪ d̪	t d			k g	q ɢ	ʔ
fric.	ɸ β	f v	θ ð	s z	ʃ ʒ		x ɣ	χ ʁ	h ɦ
approx.				ɹ		j	w		
trill				r				ʀ	
flap				ɾ					
lat.				l			ɫ		

Appendix C: Basic Speech Anatomy

Location and terminology of speech production in the mouth, nose and throat

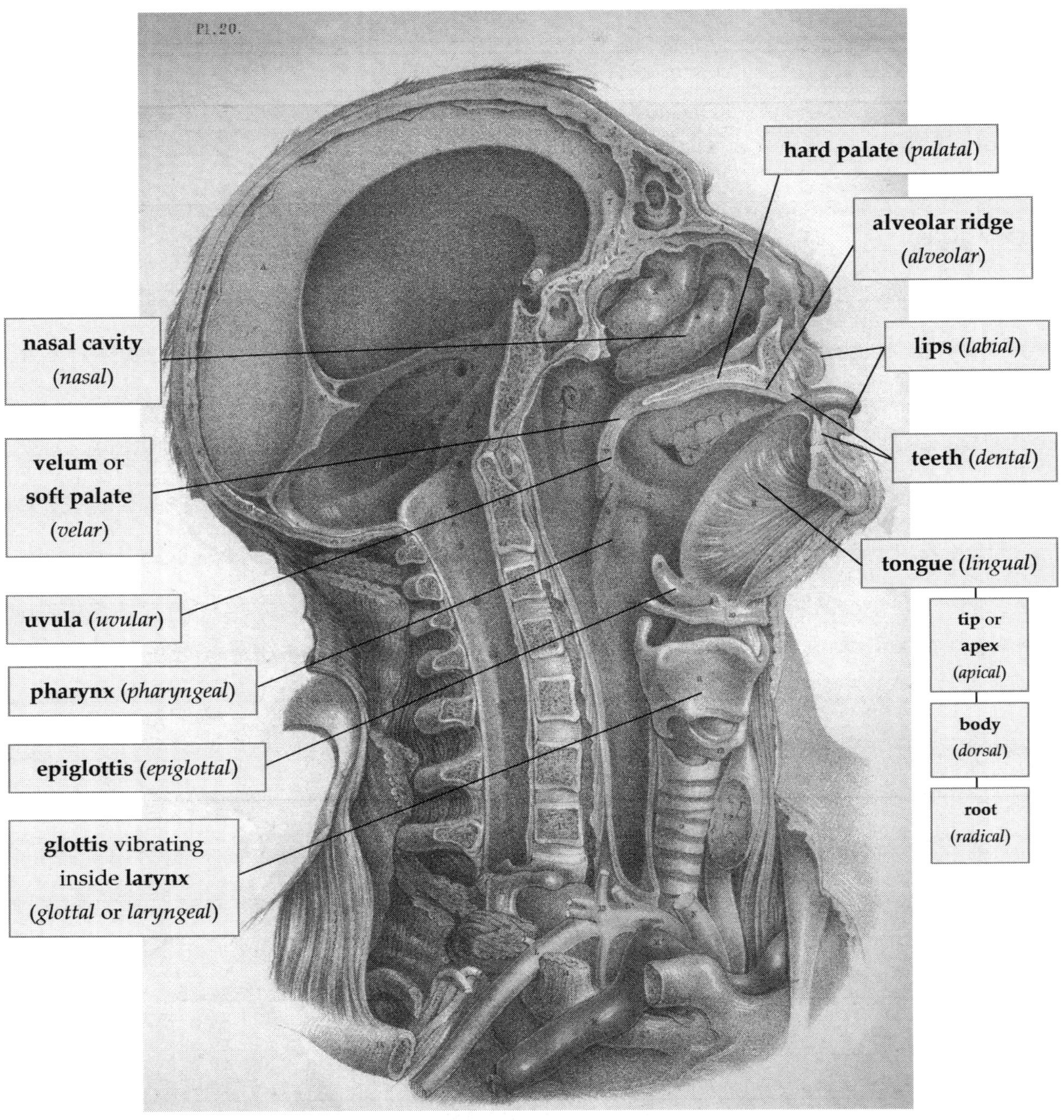

The image on this page is a faithful reproduction of lithograph plate 20 from the 1859 edition of Joseph Maclise's *Surgical Anatomy*. Indicator lines and text boxes were added by the present author.

Simplified Illustration of Vocal Anatomy

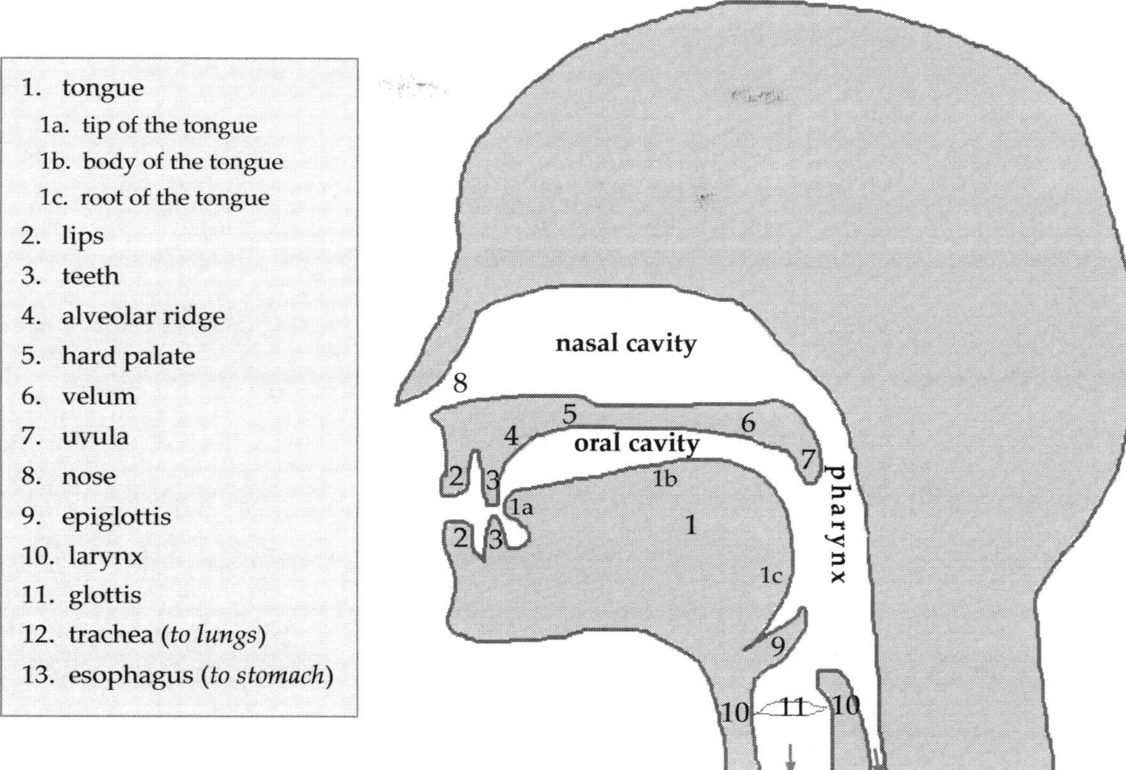

Obstruction of Oral Airflow

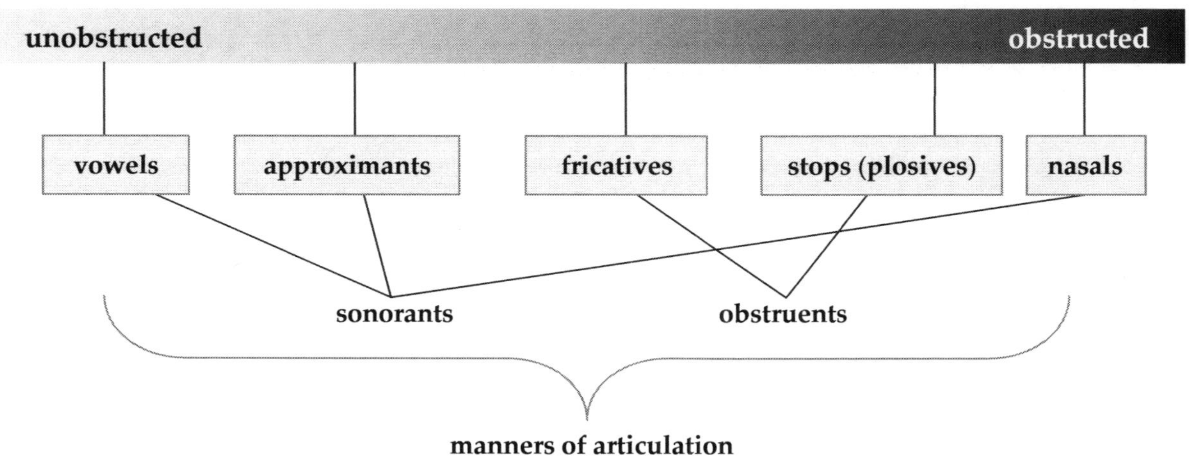

Appendix D: Answers to the Exercises

Exercise 1

1.	ago	2	ə	o		
2.	grabbing	2	æ	i		
3.	stood	1	ʊ			
4.	blunder	2	ʌ	ə		
5.	sword	1	o or ɔ			
6.	composite	3	ə	ɑ	ɪ	*(American)*
			ɒ	ə	ɪ	*(British)*
7.	phonetic	3	ə	ɛ	ɪ	
8.	taught	1	ɑ or ɔ *(American)*			
			ɔ *(British)*			
9.	arrested	3	ə	ɛ	ɪ	
10.	thickened	2	ɪ	ə		

Exercise 2

1.	love	mid, back	4.	rune	close, back
2.	did	close, front	5.	bad	open, front
3.	knead	close, front	6.	chef	mid, front

Exercise 3

1.	stʌd	stud	mid back unrounded vowel
2.	stʊd	stood	(*near-*)close (*near-*)back rounded vowel
3.	hæ̃d	hand	(*near-*)open (*near-*)front unrounded nasal vowel
4.	hiːd	heed	long close front unrounded vowel
5.	ɪz	is	(*near-*)close (*near-*)front unrounded vowel
6.	ɑf	off	open back unrounded vowel
7.	diːl	deal	long close front unrounded vowel
8.	dɛlt	dealt	mid (*near-*)front unrounded vowel
9.	spæːn	span	long (*near-*)open (*near-*)front unrounded vowel

10.	siːn	scene/seen	long close front unrounded vowel
11.	rũːm	room	long close back rounded nasal vowel
12.	piːs	peace	long close front unrounded vowel
13.	ɔːt	ought	long mid back rounded vowel
14.	piːz	peas	long close front unrounded vowel
15.	kwɪk	quick	(*near-*)close (*near-*)front unrounded vowel

Exercise 4

1.	h**ou**nd	[aʊ]	4.	**ai**sle	[aɪ]
2.	n**i**ne	[aɪ]	5.	R**o**me	[əʊ] *(British)* or [oʊ] *(American)*
3.	s**ay**	[eɪ]	6.	**ai**m	[eɪ]

Exercise 5

1.	act	ʔ	k	t	glottal, velar, alveolar
2.	ladder	l	d	ɹ	alveolar, alveolar, alveolar
3.	wink	w	ŋ	k	velar, velar, velar
4.	hauled	h	ɫ	d	glottal, alveolar, alveolar
5.	reason	ɹ	z	n	alveolar, alveolar, alveolar
6.	every	ʔ	v	ɹ	glottal, labiodental, alveolar
7.	ration	ɹ	ʃ	n	alveolar, postalveolar, alveolar
8.	ridged	ɹ	dʒ	d	alveolar, postalveolar, alveolar
9.	faced	f	s	t	labiodental, alveolar, alveolar
10.	using	j	z	ŋ	palatal, alveolar, velar
11.	houses	h	z	z	glottal, alveolar, alveolar
12.	think	θ	ŋ	k	dental, velar, velar
13.	washed	w	ʃ	t	velar, postalveolar, alveolar
14.	bathes	b	ð	z	bilabial, dental, alveolar
15.	aches	ʔ	k	s	glottal, velar, alveolar

Exercise 6

1.	act	ʔ	k	t	plosive, plosive, plosive
2.	ladder	l	d	ɹ	lateral, plosive, approximant
3.	wink	w	ŋ	k	approximant, nasal, plosive
4.	hauled	h	ɫ	d	fricative, lateral, plosive
5.	reason	ɹ	z	n	approximant, fricative, nasal
6.	every	ʔ	v	ɹ	plosive, fricative, approximant
7.	ration	ɹ	ʃ	n	approximant, fricative, nasal
8.	ridged	ɹ	dʒ	d	approximant, affricate, plosive
9.	faced	f	s	t	fricative, fricative, plosive
10.	using	j	z	ŋ	approximant, fricative, nasal
11.	houses	h	z	z	fricative, fricative, fricative
12.	think	θ	ŋ	k	fricative, nasal, plosive
13.	washed	w	ʃ	t	approximant, fricative, plosive
14.	bathes	b	ð	z	plosive, fricative, fricative
15.	aches	ʔ	k	s	plosive, plosive, fricative

Exercise 7

1.	runs	/	rats	[z] / [s]
2.	tints	/	adds	[s] / [z]
3.	apple	/	lab	[p] / [b]
4.	ruined	/	crashed	[d] / [t]
5.	the	/	thing	[ð] / [θ]
6.	lock	/	grain	[k] / [g]
7.	range	/	crutch	[dʒ] / [tʃ]
8.	off	/	of	[f] / [v]
9.	shiny	/	lesion	[ʃ] / [ʒ]
10.	match	/	nudging	[tʃ] / [dʒ]

Exercise 8

1. [dajm]
2. [stijd]
3. [fjuw]
4. [bɹ̩d]
5. [lɪɾl̩] *(American)* or [lɪʔl̩] *(British)*
6. [pɹ̩sn̩]
7. [kʰeɪm]
8. [æpʰ]
9. [tʰaɪm]

Exercise 9

1.	d / d̪	place of articulation
	ʔ / ɹ	place of articulation, manner of articulation & voicing
	t / θ	place & manner of articulation
	χ / ɢ	manner of articulation & voicing
	w / l	place & manner of articulation
	l / h	place of articulation, manner of articulation & voicing
	v / ɸ	place of articulation & voicing
	ŋ / w	manner of articulation

2. In a new column inserted between uvular and glottal.

3. **p̪** and **b̪** (voiceless and voiced labiodental plosives).

4. If the aspiration came to influence the articulation of the plosive (perhaps due to the speaker's timing), eventually the sound represented could have changed into a fricative (under the influence of fricative /h/) instead of an aspirated stop. In this case, the outcome might be something like a bilabial fricative for ɸ and a dental fricative for θ, precisely the sounds they represent in IPA.

Exercise 10

1. Answers will vary. Example: /d/ in "dog" and /b/ in "bat".

2. For some American speakers, /d/ has the allophone [d] in "dog" and [dʒ] in "drag".

3. i. British English [bɛtʰə] and [bɛʔə] ([tʰ] varies with [ʔ]). Phoneme: /t/

ii. [ʔ] can occur for /t/ at the end of a word, as in "spot", but not at the beginning of a word, as in "tops", where only [t^{h}] is allowed. Here [t^{h}] and [ʔ] are in complementary distribution. Phoneme: /t/

iii. /d/ in "dog" and /b/ in "bat" offer an example of contrastive distribution.

Exercise 11

Refer to the answers for Exercise 10.

Exercise 12

Answers will vary. Example: your phonemes might include /v/ and /w/, and your minimal pairs might include /waɪn/ and /vaɪn/, which prove that /v/ and /w/ are indeed distinct phonemes in English.

Exercise 13

1.	[stʌmp^{h}]	CCVCC	4.	[tʃuw]	CVC
2.	[fjiw]	CCVC	5.	[speɪd]	CCVVC
3.	[ʔown]	CVCC	6.	[daʊn]	CVVC

Exercise 14

1. [(st)ʌ(mp^{h})]
   [(f)jiw] or [(fj)i(w)]
   [(ʔ)ow(n)]
   [(tʃ)u(w)]
   [(sp)eɪ(d)]
   [(d)aʊ(n)]

2. "hurt", "butt**on**" and "handle" may contain syllabic consonants for some English speakers.

Exercise 15

1. [hu.na]
2. [ʔaː.ke.ʔa.ke.ʔa]

3. [hu.mu.hu.mu.nu.ku.nu.ku.a.pu.a.ʔa]

4. [ho.loi.mu.a]

5. [wa.la.kiː.keː]

6. [ha.wai.ʔi]

7. [paː.paː]

8. [ku.ae.hu]

9. [vai.kiː.kiː]

10. [a.lo.ha]

Exercise 16

1. [deɪ] / [deɪz], [deɪt] / [deɪts], [meɪd] / [meɪdz], [ɹeɪk] / [ɹeɪks], [ɹæːg] / [ɹæːgz]

    i. Two allophones: [s] after voiceless phonemes, [z] after voiced phonemes (including vowels).

    ii. Phoneme /s/ underlies "plural –s".

    iii. Pronounce /s/ as [s] following voiceless consonants and [z] following voiced consonant or vowel phonemes.

2. input/into, helped/healed, easy/just

    i. /n/, /d/, /s/

    ii. /n/ has [m] and [n]. /d/ has [t] and [d]. /s/ has [z] and [s].

    iii. [m] differs from [n] in place of articulation (bilabial vs. alveolar); adjacent /p/ is also bilabial. [t] differs from [d] in voicing (voiceless vs. voiced); adjacent /p/ is also voiceless. [z] differs from [s] in voicing (voiced vs. voiceless); adjacent vowels /i/ and /i/ are also voiced.

    iv. In each case, assimilation was triggered by an immediately adjacent phoneme. In /n/ + /p/, /n/ took on the place of articulation of /p/ and became [m]. In /p/ + /d/, /d/ took on the voicing of /p/ and became [t]. In /i/ + /s/ + /i/, /s/ took on the voicing of /i/ and became [z].

Exercise 17

Compare your transcriptions to these examples:

1. /ʌʔʌðætsnɑtɹaɪt/, / sɑɹikʊdjuseɪðætəgeɪn/, /ðidʒʌdʒdəsaɪdədɪnfeɪvəɹʌvðipleɪntɪf/, /aɪ ɹiːliː mɪs həɹ/
2. [ʔʌ̃ʔʌ̃ːðæʔtsnɑʔɹaɪʔ], [sɑːɹiːkʰʊdʒəseɪðæɾəgɪn], [ðədʒʌdʒdəsaɪɾɪɾɪnfeɪvəɹʌvðəpʰleɪnɪf], [ʔaɪ ɹiːliː mɪs həɹ]
3. [ˈʔʌ̃ˌʔʌ̃ːˈðæʔtsnɑʔˈɹaɪʔ], [ˈsɑːɹiˌkʰʊdʒəˈseɪðæɾəˈgɪn], [ðəˈdʒʌdʒdəˈsaɪɾɪɾɪnˈfeɪvəɹ ˌʔʌvðəˈpʰleɪnɪf], [ʔaɪˈɹiːliːˈmɪshəɹ]
4. [↗ˈʔʌ̃↘ˌʔʌ̃ː↗ˈðæʔts↘nɑʔˈɹaɪʔ], [↗ˈsɑː↘ɹiˌkʰʊdʒəˈseɪðæɾə↗ˈgɪn], [ðə↗ˈdʒʌdʒdəˈsaɪɾɪɾɪn↘ˈfeɪvəɹ ˌʔʌvðəˈ↗pʰleɪ↘nɪf], [ʔaɪ↗ˈɹiːliːˈmɪs↘həɹ]

Exercise 18

Compare your transcription to this example:

[ˈðæʔ ˌwʌzənʔ ə ˈstoʊɹ ˈɹɑbəˌɹij ˈðæʔ ˌwʌz ən əˌsæsɪˈneɪʃən ˈðæʔ ˌwʌzənʔ ə ˈkʰləɹkʰ ˈðæʔ ˌwʌz ə ˈwaɪz ˈgaɪ haʊ duw ˈaɪ ˌnoʊ jiʊ kʰəd ˈsej aɪ ˈspɛnʔ ə ˈlɪɾl̩ ˈtʰaɪm wɪθ ðə ˌʔɛfbiːˈaɪz ˈoɹgəˌnaɪzd ˈkʰɹaɪm ˌjiʊnɪʔ jiʊ ˈkʰʊd ˌseɪ ðɛɾ aɪm ˈʔɪntʰɪmɪʔliː ˈnɑlɪdʒəbl̩ wɪθ ðə ˈɹeɪŋkʰəɹɪs ˈwəɹkiŋz əv ðə ˈmɑːb ɪn ðə ˈmɪdwɛs ˈsɛkʃən əv ðɪs ˈkʰʌntʃɹiː ʔaɪd ˈlʊk ˌɪntu ɪʔ ˈpəɹsənəˌliː bʌɾ ˈaɪ gɑɾ ə ˈdeɪʔ təˈnaɪʔ]

Exercise 19

(Notice that the IPA represents affected speech.) Compare your transcription to this example:

[bʌʔ ðætʰ hiː wɒz ˈnɒʔ tʰu ˌbiː wɪˈθaʊtʰ ˈʔɪgnjəɹəns ɔː ˈprɛdʒʊdɪs mɪsˈteɪkʰən fɔː ɹeɪ ˈdʒɛntl̩mən maɪ ˈfɑːðə ˈstʰɹɒŋliː ʔəˈsɛvəˌɹeɪts bɪˈkʰɒz ɪtʰ ɪz eɪ ˈpʰɹɪnsɪpl̩ ʔɒv ˈhɪz ðætʰ ˈnəʊ ˌmæːn huː wɒz ˈnɒtʰ ʔeɪ ˈtʰɹuː ˈdʒɛntl̩mən ætʰ ˈhɑːtʰ ˈʔɛvə ˌwɒz sɪns ðiː ˈwɜːɫd bɪˈgæːn ʔeɪ ˈtʰɹuː ˈdʒɛntl̩mən ɪn ˈmæːnə hiː ˌseɪz ˈnəʊ ˈvɑːnɪʃ kʰæːn ˈhaɪd ðiː ˈgreɪn ʔɒv ðiː ˈwʊd æːnd ðætʰ ðiː ˈmɔː ˈvɑːnɪʃ juː ˈpʰʊtʰ ˈɒn ðiː ˈmɔː ðiː ˈgreɪn wɪɫ ʔɛkˈspɹɛs ʔɪtˈsɛɫf]

Index

Made in the USA
Lexington, KY
23 April 2017